Donna Kakonge

Spiderwoman

Donna Kakonge grew up in Toronto and trained as a journalist at Carleton University in Ottawa, Canada from 1990 to 1994. Her first attempt at fiction was in 1989 at the age of 17 after reading many Danielle Steele and Stephen King novels, as well as Sweet Valley

High books geared to teenagers. She did not publish this book later titled *My Roxanne* until 2007. She has written many freelance articles and reviews for newspapers, magazines and online work. Her first published short story that came out of a creative writing workshop at Carleton University with Tom Henighan was for Headlight Anthology - a Concordia University student-published journal. Kakonge did her master of arts in media studies at Concordia University from 1997 to 1999. She has taught at Carleton University as a teaching assistant, as well as Concordia

University. She has also taught a full responsibility course at Concordia University and overseas at Makerere University in Kampala, Uganda. From 2006 to present, Kakonge teaches at Centennial College, Seneca College, the University of Guelph-Humber and Humber College all in Toronto. She has worked as a journalist on and off with the Canadian Broadcasting Corporation from 1992 to 2007. She received a student award from Carleton University as the graduating student with the most promise of becoming an exceptional journalist in honour of the late journalist Marjorie Nichols. She has also received a Gemini nomination for a pilot of a television show that aired on the Discovery Channel, plus numerous scholarships to attend the Innoversity Diversity Summit in Toronto. She has also received a Quebecor Documentary Fellowship. Kakonge is also the author of *What Happened to the Afro?, How to Write Creative Non-fiction, Spiderwoman*, editor of *Being Healthy: Selected Works from the Internet, Do Not Know, My Story of Transportation, Draft*, a CD of radio documentaries called "Nine,"

5   Spiderwoman by Donna Kay C. Kakonge

Journalism Stories Collection, Digital Journals and Numerology and two audio stories from Spiderwoman, the story "Matoke" and "Church Sunday." The latter appeared in Headlight Anthology Donna Kakonge lives in Toronto, Canada.

www.donnakakonge.com

BOOKS AND CDS BY DONNA KAKONGE

What Happened to the Afro?

How to Write Creative Non-fiction

Spiderwoman

My Roxanne

Being Healthy: Selected Works from the Internet (edited by)

Do Not Know

My Story of Transportation

Draft

"Nine" (CD)

Journalism Stories Collection

7   Spiderwoman by Donna Kay C. Kakonge
  Digital Journals and Numerology

"Matoke" (Audio Download)

"Spiderwoman" (Audio Download)

In My Pocket

In My Pocket
Spiderwoman

Donna Kakonge

Lulu.com

Spiderwoman by Donna Kay C. Kakonge

FIRST EDITION LULU INTERNATIONAL EDITION, May 2007

Copyright 2007 by Donna Kay Kakonge, M.A.

All rights researched under International and Pan-American Copyright Conventions.

Published in the United States by Lulu.com.

National Archives of Canada Cataloguing in Publication Data

Kakonge, Donna

10 Spiderwoman by Donna Kay C. Kakonge
Spiderwoman

ISBN: 978-0-9783738-2-5
9798518829206

Book Design by Dreamstime.com

Manufactured in the United States.

11 Spiderwoman by Donna Kay C. Kakonge

To Oshun

Spiderwoman

By Donna Kay C. Kakonge

13 Spiderwoman by Donna Kay C. Kakonge

Table of Contents

Matoke – 3

Church Sunday – 6

Lizard in the Yard – 20

Three Quarters – 36

Chicoutimi – 60

Elephant Woman – 68

14 Spiderwoman by Donna Kay C. Kakonge

Spiderwoman – 83

Black Hair - 90

This is dedicated to all the good people in my life, including you, the reader.

Matoke

In the early 1980's, when I was 10 years old, things changed at my school with the arrival of a new vice-principal. At O'Connor Public School in Toronto, Mr. Goldberg set up a close-circuit television studio. The show the students and Mr. Goldberg produced was called *OCTV News*.

In a small room of the school that used to be the teachers' lounge, coffee makers and plastic cushions were replaced by an anchor's desk and a camera as big as me. A few grade five students, myself included, rotated through the various production jobs. Sometimes I was the sound engineer, which meant putting the needle on the Beatles song, "Here Comes the Sun" – our theme music. Sometimes I was the announcer, which meant telling Angelikki to show up to the Peter Pan play rehearsals. She was playing Peter, and I was Wendy.

One "International Day," we had to bring a dish from our heritage to be sampled by other students. Mr. Goldberg forgot it was International Day and didn't write anything into our scripts about it for the *OCTV News*. That day I was co-announcing.

"Susan and Eric, just ad-lib about the International Day after the news," Mr. Goldberg said seconds before we went on-air.

After the news, Eric asked me what dish I had brought in and I told him "matoke" – a common Ugandan meal made of steamed and mashed green bananas.

"Where is Uganda?" Eric asked.

"In Africa," I said.

"Oh, Africa! I thought they ate people there, I didn't know they ate food!" Eric said.

I almost burst into tears.

"I think there's a lot you don't know about Africa, Eric," I said. "My uncles, aunts and cousins who still live there don't eat people."

19 Spiderwoman by Donna Kay C. Kakonge

"Well what is Africa like?" he asked.

I had only been to Uganda as a baby; I was born and raised in Canada.

My father came to Canada on a Commonwealth scholarship. When he returned to Uganda for a new job with a new wife and baby (that was me), Dictator Idi Amin was in power. We all escaped the country with only our lives.

I told Eric - and also about 500 other students

who were watching *OCTV* - everything I knew about Uganda. I told them stories about my family who lived in a brick house, not a grass hut; who drove cars, not camels, and who ate matoke, rather than people. The response was phenomenal. Scores of students wanted to know more. They had questions, many of which I could not answer. I asked my teacher if my father could come to class and talk about Uganda. Soon afterwards, Dad was standing at the front of the class with my globe piggy bank, rattling change as he turned it to point out Uganda.

21 Spiderwoman by Donna Kay C. Kakonge

My father said we fed those students with knowledge of African people. I guess we did feed those kids at O'Connor a lot more than matoke.

CHURCH SUNDAY

I held my Granny's hand as we walked down the street to the church for the last Sunday. We were on a northbound Toronto street heading uphill to an eastbound avenue. The bakery behind us was masking the smell of garbage as we passed by the stuffed green and black bags balanced on the curb. Sweat spotted my temples. It was hot for an August morning before global warming. Ever since Granny had come from St.Vincent & the Grenadines, It was like she had brought the heat with her. I couldn't remember a hotter summer. She was panting with every step. She never wanted to admit that the walk to the church was hard for her, so she complained about everything else instead.

"All this hardness does hurt me feet," she said, pounding a foot on the concrete like I didn't know that it was hard.

"Do you want to walk on the grass?"

"Da grass kills bugs," she said pointing to the

pesticide sign. "Me nah want me feet pun dat."

I sighed. "Do you want me to carry you?"

"I too fat. You would die from me weight."

Granny laughed softly at her comment. We were at the candy store on the top of the hill, where the long-leg man once lived. The man owned a store on the first floor of his house and he had one leg longer than the other. He said it was because he had "one foot in the grave." My bike gang and I used to hang outside of his store and he would chase us away, telling us we were bad for business. I never really understood that because we were usually the only ones who ever came into the store. We thought for sure he was rich from the profit of selling Popeye cigarettes 20 cents more than anybody else. But, the store was empty now, so I bought my candy from across the street. The building was waiting for a new owner, and I just hoped whoever it was would treat the neighbourhood kids better.

26 Spiderwoman by Donna Kay C. Kakonge

This being Granny's fourth Sunday in Toronto, it was only the fourth time I saw Granny wearing a dress where the colours were not faded. The lace-trimmed neckline was scooped low enough to see her gold cross pendant. This Sunday, Granny's dress was in yellow and kept her bosom in place. She wore her shined white shoes which she worked to keep clean by sidestepping a few pothole puddles from last night's rain. She had a white hand bag to match, and in her other hand was her Holy Bible with its black cover and words in gold.

27 Spiderwoman by Donna Kay C. Kakonge

Granny's hair was free from the green and gold scarf she usually wore and was pressed and curled up at the ends. The only everyday-thing that Granny wore on Sundays was her knee-highs, the same brown ones she wore everyday, no matter how hot it was.

"Ya legs just can't be naked, gal," she told me as she insisted I wear stockings.

An hour after Granny arrived; she spent 10 minutes giving me and my mother the mangoes and pomegranates she had smuggled through customs. She also asked me about school, although I wasn't even in school. Then she spent 50 minutes filling my mother in on all the gossip on every Vincentian my mother did and didn't know. With her last word on whether or not my Auntie Pansy was going crazy because she kept her Christmas tree up all year. Granny congratulated my mother on divorcing my father and asked where the church was. I had stopped going to church years ago, but I went on holidays with my mother.

29 Spiderwoman by Donna Kay C. Kakonge

My mother sent Granny to our Easter and Christmas church, a Methodist one which we needed to take a "nasty bus" as Granny called it. Sunday was the only day my mother got to sleep more than four hours, so she forced me to go with Granny. Now I was stuck with this Sunday chore.

Granny hated the Methodist church, it made her fall asleep. She said there were too many white people and she couldn't stand organ music that was played with more than one mistake. The Monday after that first Sunday, when the sun was burning at the top of the sky, she said she was going for a walk. She didn't come back till the moon was up. But, she found a Black Baptist church which was walking distance from my mother's house.

"We naw need to step on dat nasty bus, Susan," she said.

She grinned, but her plate wasn't in so I could see her tongue through the spaces in her teeth.

Spiderwoman by Donna Kay C. Kakonge

"The bus isn't that bad, Granny," I said.

"Too many white people."

Granny just wasn't used to white people like I was. Granny had been to every Caribbean country, to Brazil, Panama, and she had even been to Ghana, but this was her first time in a country north of the equator. My mother had lived in Canada for over 20 years, and even she still wasn't used to white people. She always complained about them at work.

About how they would ask her stupid questions about the food she brought for lunch, and about her hair.

Now Granny was here to help my mother complain about white people. Granny had been diagnosed with breast cancer before I even understood what it was. In June, her doctors removed a breast six days before her 75th birthday. My mother sent her a card with an airline ticket in it.

The Baptist church on Davenport was brown

33 Spiderwoman by Donna Kay C. Kakonge

  brick with three floors under a black roof. Like every Sunday, we saw a black woman standing outside the door. She only had one leg, her right one, and she had a crutch under her left arm. I occasionally sneaked some looks at her; I didn't want her to think I was staring. She had a red scarf wrapped around her head, and tufts of kinky hair sticking out. As we approached I stared at her right ear. It was the only part of her skin which was white. On our first church Sunday I asked Granny why the woman's ear was like that.

"That show how these white people here are just hole' in her by de ear," she said.

I laughed and asked my mother when we got home.

"Must be some kind of burn or something, or frostbite. That kind of thing can take the colour right out of you," my mother said.

The woman with the crutch had a blue furry coat on, and the fur was wearing away at her elbows. I wondered why she wasn't fainting from the heat. Her face was dry. Her cheeks were plump and the skin looked grey and cracked. Her cheeks were so high on her face that her eyes seemed to squint as if they were trying to see over them. The coat hung to her waist and a white skirt blew around her leg from the breeze. It was sheer and I could see her red underwear, and the stump of her left leg. Her foot was bare and her toes curled and bent against the concrete. On the ground by her foot were pink stains and a Popsicle stick. The ants were crawling onto her toes, but she didn't seem to mind it.

"Honey, how ya feeling?" Granny asked the woman.

I pulled at Granny's arm, hoping she would walk past the woman, ignoring her. Granny's the first person who I had ever seen talk to a street person. The woman smiled at Granny without showing her teeth. She held out her hand to us, her eyes fixed on our shoes. Granny opened her purse and gave the woman $5.00. She had given the woman $10.00 last week.

Spiderwoman by Donna Kay C. Kakonge

"Sorry, I don't have a lickle bit more today, sweetheart."

The woman closed her hand around the five and kept staring at the ground.

The woman said nothing; she didn't even look at Granny. I pressed Granny's hand and pulled her through the church doors, relieved to get away from her.

"Granny you shouldn't give people like that so much of your money," I said once we were behind the church doors. "You just don't know what they'll do with it."

Every other time I said that to Granny she just ignored me. That day she told me that she should take me back to St. Vincent with her. There was no way I would allow that to happen. I had been to St.Vincent before, and it was hot and boring, and even their big city called Kingstown was rural.

Granny and I found a pew near the front. She needed to get up close to see. The church was packed. Those Sundays were among the few times in my life when I saw so many black people all in the same place. I was in awe.

When the choir and band started, there was hardly enough room to dance in the pew. I didn't mind so much going to this church because of the choir and the band. Every church song was uplifted with the pounding of a piano, a few saxophone solos and a drum beat. The choir would do `Four Tops' moves to the music, raising their hands when they sang "up" and hugging themselves when they sang "Jesus loves me, this I know". That band played the songs of God so well, every butt got out of its seat and wiggled to the beat. Granny shook her butt and her yellow dress just shimmied. She raised her arms up to her bosom and she clapped so hard the wind from her hands made the feather on her hat wave. Granny's voice was so good; she should have been in the choir. When she sang, her top lip would curl, looking like it was trying to reach her nose, but it never did. Her lip curled like that when she smiled too. My lip curls like that too when I smile. I don't really like to dance in public, but even I shook my shoulders and shuffled my feet a bit.

When the music stopped it was time for the preacher to speak. He waited for everybody to catch their breath. When he started, he spoke louder than the music, to keep people awake I figured. Occasionally Granny would scream "Amen" to things the preacher said or stand-up and yell "Yesuh." Other older men and women would do this too. When the preacher read from the scriptures, Granny opened up her Holy Bible, extending it to me so we could follow along together. I pretended to follow, but I just stared at the page and yawned. Once my yawning started, it wouldn't stop. Granny stared at the preacher like he was Moses walking on water. It was the look in her eyes that made me not tell her that I smelled liquor on the preacher's breath when he kissed me on the cheek when I first met him.

After the service, Granny said goodbye to the preacher. Walking out of the church always seemed difficult for her, but this time was worse. She dragged her feet, still singing the church songs softly to herself. The walk back was faster going downhill. We crossed the street and came to the shortcut leading to the block of townhouses where I lived. Granny stopped walking.

"I don't have me Bible."

I looked at her, all over her. "Are you sure? Check your purse."

"I know I don't have me Bible," she said without checking her purse. "I must have left it at de church."

I didn't want to go all the way back there, especially with how slow Granny walked. Also I couldn't wait to get home. I was breathing heat.

"Lawd, Richard done give me dat Bible. I can't lose it."

Richard was my grandfather who I had never even met. He died two years before I was born.

"Okay, Granny, just go home," I said and turned around. "I'll run back and get it for you."

I was already running when I heard her thanking me. Once I reached the candy store, I was panting out so much hot air I stopped. I got to the church doors so quick it surprised me. I had never realized how close the church was without walking with Granny. I could hear singing inside and guessed it was the choir practicing. I didn't want to disturb them so I tried to enter quietly.

I noticed then how big the room was without all those people in it. When I glanced on the small stage where the choir was, nobody was there. But in a front pew, I saw the back of the woman with the crutch.

"Jesus loves me, this I know . . . " she sang.

One hand was grasped around the crutch, and the other was suspended in the air, the fingers wiggling double time to her singing.

". . .cuz the Bible tells me so. . ."

She shook her hips, leaning on the crutch. She would occasionally stick out her bum and shake it.

I didn't know what to do. I tried to look around to see if I saw the Bible anywhere near, but I knew I might have to come right behind the woman to get it. I thought about coming back, but I didn't want Granny's Bible to get stolen. Who would take a Bible in a church, I asked myself. I wasn't sure, but I thought maybe somebody could.

I kept taking a few steps forward, then stopping, hoping the woman wouldn't turn around. The closer I got to her, the more my stomach was knotting. I didn't want to see her. I was halfway there, wondering whether I should just wait outside until I saw her leave. She stopped dancing and turned around.

I looked past her.

"I'm sorry," I said, darting my eyes to her. "My Granny forgot something."

I wanted to dash to find the Bible, get it and just run away. The woman shifted her weight on the crutch and bent forward. She was trying to pick up something from the seat in front of her. It was the Bible. It took a while for her to grasp the book without dropping it. She held it out to me.

I came close enough to smell the scent of the streets from her. I felt sickness in my throat.

I held my breath and grabbed the book from her. I darted my eyes to her, her eyes were squinty, but I knew she was staring at me.

Then she held out her hand.

I didn't have a purse or any pockets. I didn't have anything to give her.

"I'm sorry," I said and I ran out of the church.

I didn't care that the sweat stung my eyes as

I ran home. I approached the house and saw Granny out on the veranda, sitting on a mahogany chair.

"Why you crying, gal,"

"I'm not," I said wiping my face.

"Something did trouble ya."

She wouldn't let me go inside until I told her. I sat in a lawn chair with purple and green stripes. I had the Holy Bible in my hand.

When I finished telling her, she took the Bible from me and held it in the air, shaking it.

"You should have given her de Bible," she said.

LIZARD IN THE YARD

On the dirt road children walk bare-footed and chickens are loose from their cages on the volcanic isle of St.Vincent. The silence was a distraction.

My mind was flitting about, like a flirtatious girl's hair. I looked out from the porch and didn't see pigeons, or streetlights, or concrete sidewalks. I realised how much I missed home.

A plane ticket to St. Vincent was a 14th birthday gift from my grandmother. I thought it would be pleasant to see her, but in fact I looked forward to the few days left. I would not even look out the airplane window until I could see Toronto.

Granny lived in a small bungalow painted in peach, and inside it always smelled like codfish. Although it was always sunny outside, in Granny's house it was dark. She had sheers and heavy green velour drapes on the windows that were usually drawn. When I asked her if she could let in a little light, Granny would draw the green drapes open and splashes of luminance came through the sheers... fuzzy.

I spent most of my days sitting in the living room trying to get a clear picture on the small Sears television set given to Granny by my mother. St.Vincent got their television shows mainly from Barbados, and there wasn't much to watch. Since I had been in St.Vincent, I had watched the Agatha Christie movie "Evil Under the Sun" three times.

"Why don't you go for a walk?" Granny asked.

The idea worried me. I had been there for a week and had never gone anywhere by myself. I kept having visions of a wild animal attacking. I had spent another day getting only as far out of the house as the porch. A walk would be good for my skinny legs. I just was not used to the heat in St.Vincent. Although Granny's place was hot, it was still better than outside.

The nights were cooler, so I decided to visit Aunt Pansy and see if she was home. She lived just down the road and I hadn't seen her since I'd been in St. Vincent. Granny had told me she was in the hospital for being "funny upstairs."

I let Granny know I was taking a walk and hit the street, or brown dirt path.

The air was so hot and thick, its heat molested me. I followed the road, occasionally wiping the sweat from my eyes. I followed the bend in the road and passed in between two houses where I heard singing.

The tune wasn't familiar, but it sounded like a calypso song. I walked towards the sound wondering who it could be singing so loudly. The voice sounded young and sweet, like a child's.

There was a rickety brown fence that looked like it was put up with scrap pieces of wood to protect a backyard. The singing was coming from the other side. I didn't want to climb the fence because it looked like it would fall down. I walked around it. On one side, I saw an opening. I started to walk to it, ducking my head to avoid the low hanging leaves of a tree. I made it to the hole in the fence.

"Jump up, jump up!" the woman sang jumping. "Ya got to shake to de beat, shake it, shake it . . ."

Every time she said shake it, the broom was tucked to her chest as her shoulders wiggled. With one hand she grasped the broom and shook it so hard the wood handle looked like rubber.

I decided to visit my aunt later. I began to crawl and felt something scurry down my back. I jumped up and shook, trying to whip off whatever it was on my spine.

Turning around and barrelling through the hole in the fence, I fell. The thing had now crawled underneath my dress. I rolled around on the grass, desperately grasping at my back, trying to catch the thing.

"Hole on," I heard. I kept rolling, unable to keep still while the thing kept crawling.

"I tell you I can't kill the thing if you don't stop moving."

I dug my fingers into the grass, keeping as still as I could.

"Hurry," I said.

"Git on ya belly."

I lied on my stomach, trying to keep my face away from the grass. Its smell offended me. I could feel the dirt in my nails.

I felt a foot hit my back in the spot where the crawling was, then felt nothing.

"Is it off?"

"Yeah."

I sprang to my feet then watched the woman

go after what was crawling on my back. I walked behind her, watching her stalking the little animal which was scurrying through the grass. Pansy held the broom in the air, towering over the animal, as I leaned over her shoulder, I could see it was a lizard. I shuddered.

The lizard came out of the grass and ran across the concrete towards Pansy's back door. Pansy brought down her broom on top of the lizard. She hit it and I turned away, not wanting to see its destruction. I heard three other thumps, then silence.

"He's dead," Aunt Pansy said.

She bent down and picked something up.

"You want da tail?"

She dangled a little green piece of lizard flesh in my face. I took a step back quickly.

"No."

Pansy shook her head.

"The tail grows back you know? The lizard is lucky, he lose and get back."

I looked at the squished lizard on Aunt Pansy's concrete thinking there would be no tail growing back on this one, then I looked at my Aunt. Aunt Pansy eyed the tail, looked at me, and then brought the tail to her mouth. She licked it.

"I think this'll be sweet in my soup."

My stomach felt queasy. A funny taste was in my throat. It felt like bile.

"Ya look sick, chile. I tell ya joke, me a joke wit'cha."

I looked at her and noticed she was wearing makeup. Underneath all of that was my Aunt Pansy. Her lashes looked long and fake, and so heavy I was surprised she could keep her eyes open as wide as they were. On her eyelids and under her painted black brows was a frosty purple. On her cheeks were two large circles of red which matched the shiny glossy colour on her lips. Her lips looked so wet. Her grey hair, streaked with black was twisted on her head.

I tried to smile weakly at her joke, still feeling sick and unable to let go of my stomach.

"I've got ease for ya belly," she turned and walked to her back door. "Come."

I hesitated.

Aunt Pansy walked to the back door and looked over her shoulder to see me still standing in the same place. She went through the door, disappearing inside, but left the door open.

Could it be true that she worshipped the devil? Granny said that's why she was "funny upstairs." I peered through her door, and wanted to see inside. It was getting dark, the sky was red and purple. I couldn't stay long any way.

The first thing that hit me about the house was the smell. It was of shortbread cookies, my favourite. It was saner than codfish. The house was small, from where I stood at the door; I could see the whole place except for what was down the hallway, which to my guess would be a bathroom. The floors looked dusty and like they were made of a dirty brown wood. Her living room had a fancy sofa with the plastic still on. A small coffee table had picture frames all over it, some in gold, and some in silver. I could not see from the door the pictures in the frames. In the corner of the room was an artificial Christmas tree, kept standing by red metal poles, each gripped into the plastic trunk of the tree? It was decorated with silver apples and red bells which looked like they were made out of wrinkled paper. There were pale yellow lights on the tree, which were the only lights on in the room. On top of the tree was an angel with a black face. She was in the kitchen, beckoning me to come in.

There were two large black dolls across from

the rocking chair. They looked like brother and sister. The boy doll had short curls and denim overalls and the girl doll had two curly ponytails stuck above her ears and a short-sleeved denim dress. Their large eyes looked alive and I had to look at them carefully to see that they were glass.

"Those are my babies," she said. "Just seat dem on the sofa, dey want ta listen to the radio now any ways."

I picked them up and moved past the

Christmas tree to seat them on the sofa.

"They're cute," I said.

"Yes."

"What are their names?"

"Peas n' Rice?"

I sat in the rocking chair and turned to look at the dolls.

"Peas n' Rice?"

"Yeah, the girl is Rice, her favourite thing to eat."

I moved my eyes away from the dolls and looked at the tree.

"It's pretty, eh?" Pansy asked.

"Yes, it is." Christmas all year round? I wondered.

"I like pretty things."

I looked at her. Well, she was definitely eccentric, but so far I could see no signs of devil-worship.

"I was baking before, I making shortbread cookies. Once I done these, dey'll be in de oven and baked in no time, ya'll have some."

"No, that's okay," I said, not wanting to accept any food.

"They'll make ya belly feel nice," she said kneading the dough. "Ya too thin anyways, ya'll have some Pansy cookies and feel nice. Ya Granny's cooking can't be good."

Pansy stood up and then picked up a tray of star-shaped unbaked cookies.

"Dem cookies must be done by now. Hole on. Ya belly will feel sweet soon."

She disappeared into the kitchen.

From where I sat at the dining room table, a large oak buffet covered the wall. Within its frame it had oak drawers on the bottom; I couldn't see how many from where I sat, because the table cut off my view. On the top were glass doors, where inside many crystal glasses and china plates, cups and saucers were showcased. I stood up to look closer. On the middle shelf was a crystal glass with a colourless picture taped to its front. The picture was of former Prime Minister of Canada, Pierre Elliott Trudeau. I thought I would have to ask Pansy about it.

I could see Pansy coming back from the kitchen with a tray of those cookies. She placed them on the table.

"Ya gonna want some milk to go wit da treats, right?"

I looked at the cookies, then at the picture on the glass.

"Sure," I said without looking at her.

Pansy went into the kitchen.

I took my first bite of a cookie as Pansy placed a tall glass of milk in front of me. My teeth sank into the shortbread and chewed the morsels, trying to keep the taste on my tongue as long as possible. I didn't even realise that Pansy had her large bottom hanging off the edge of the seat, watching me eat.

"Ya like dem?"

I nodded.

"Best I think I've ever had."

Pansy smiled so wide, exposing that she had two bottom right side teeth missing.

"Have plenty, I make plenty."

I looked up and noticed the picture in the case again.

"Pansy, why do you have a picture of Prime

Minister Trudeau?" I asked pointing to it.

Pansy spun her head to look, and then turned her head quickly back at me.

"My friend Annie sent me dat picture when she first went to Canada in 1966. Vincentians in Canada speak well of Trudeau and de Liberals. I keep it to remind me how good I got it."

"What do you mean?"

"'Fore he came minista, Canada didn't let in lots of black people. Liberals like black people. Now, plenty of Vincentians left this place and went to Canada. Ya momma went dere 'cause Trudeau let her in, so did Natalie, so did Jensen," she started kneading the dough again and I noticed that she was sniffling.

"I lost most of my loves to dat place."

"You don't like Canada, Auntie Pansy?"

"I hate it."

"How could you say that, Auntie?" I was confused. "Have you even been to Canada?"

"Just once, that was in 1967 to visit Annie. I missed her. She lived in Montreal, in a pretty place. She even had a car after only one year. But de place was so cold. I still can't get de chill out of me bones. It changed me for life, I've never been de same."

"Any ways, I wish everybody was still here,"

Pansy said. "Things were good when I could walk to any of my family's house. When you needed comfort, all ya had to do was knock on a door, and somebody be dere to love ya."

"But, my mother wants you to live with her, Auntie Pansy. She would be there for you. You don't need to be alone here."

Pansy stopped kneading the dough and just looked at me.

"But this is my place, Su-zann. I can't breathe any other air or live in any other place but here. If I left I'd be as unhappy as everybody else. I don't have a car here, but you ask ya momma if having a car makes her happy?"

I finished her cookie then looked at my watch. It was half past eight.

"I won't have any time to eat all those cookies, Aunt Pansy, I should head back to Granny's."

Aunt Pansy went into the kitchen and came back with a bag. She filled the bag with the cookies.

"Su-zann, I have something to ask you."

I nodded for her to continue.

"Do you think I'm crazy?" Aunt Pansy asked.

I didn't know how to answer. What did crazy mean any ways? Granny told me that Aunt

Pansy was like a rollercoaster, she went up and down and had been like that for as long as she could remember. Pansy probably kept the dolls because they reminded her of Natalie and Jensen, her children that were taken away from her when she got sick one time. I had never seen Aunt Pansy sick, but Granny told me it was quite a sight. Sometimes Pansy was so sick she wouldn't get out of bed and wouldn't talk and other times she was so sick you couldn't keep her down and she wouldn't stop talking. I had never seen those sides of Aunt Pansy, I just thought she was eccentric.

"I don't think your crazy, Aunt Pansy."

She smiled.

"Good."

Three Quarters

I was taking the long bus ride home in the August heat, standing beside a white girl, and pushing her hair off my brown face.

With every bump and jolt of the bus I was getting closer to the girl. Her rose-scented perfume invaded my nose and hurt my head. The bus was packed with bodies and odour. I peered through the window and saw people stomping the streets of Toronto. I watched the cars passing by, and wished that I had taken my car to the conference. But I would have had to park it in the underground garage, and I hated doing that. The smell of it made me sick.

"Ouch," I said.

The pain in my toe brought tears to my eyes. I looked down quickly to see the white girl trying to shuffle her cheap canvas shoes away from mine, which were imported from Spain.

"Watch where you put your clumsy feet," I

said.

"I'm so sorry, I'm very sorry," she said.

I examined my shoes, checking for any scuffs. Finding none, I decided to get away from the girl. Lugging my briefcase, I moved to the back of the bus, searching for a seat.

As I moved, the bus stopped and emptied out. I had no problem finding a seat. I forgot to buy the *Globe and Mail* before I got on the bus, so I chose a seat which seemed the most interesting.

I sat down, facing a girl who was talking so loud to the man sitting beside her, I couldn't help but overhear.

"I'm sick and tired of having your disgusting friends over at my house," the girl said.

"They come over, they steal food from my fridge, they fart on my couch, they hog the TV, then they steal money from me - I'm f***ing sick of it Ray."

I thought the man named Ray was going to hit the girl. Instead, he lit a cigarette, disregarding the no smoking sign at the front of the bus. He turned to the girl and slowly blew smoke into her face.

"Lay off me," he said.

The girl's face twisted in disgust. She turned away from the smoke, tossing her hair in Ray's face and moved her eyes to look out the window behind me. I watched the blonde hair settle on her bare shoulders. The hair covered her tattoo of a red rose.

Her hair was frizzy and had dark roots. Her face was tanned but looked unattractive with the scowl on it. Even from where I sat, I saw the clumps of navy blue mascara on her lashes, and a thick navy blue line on her bottom eyelid. I looked at her eyes. I felt like I had seen those eyes before.

I looked at her long straight nose, full cheeks and small mouth. Then I looked back into her eyes. I was sure I knew this girl. My mind whipped through all the classes I've had and faces I've seen in the classroom. I thought of the faces in my U of T classes and at all the hip-house, reggae and dance parties I went to. I tried to remember all the people I had worked with at Simpson's . . . at Druxy's . . . at Toys R Us . . . I thought of all the friends I had in high school - but most of the people I remembered knowing were black. My eyes hovered over her dark roots and I thought I must know this girl from way back, when I had no other choice but to associate with girls like her.

Startling me, the girl looked my way. I was caught and embarrassed, and I quickly looked away. I hid my eyes, not wanting her to recognise me before I figured out who she was.

Ray threw his cigarette butt to the ground and crushed it with a cowboy boot. The girl looked at him and he snorted.

"Whad you looking at?" he asked her.

She stuck her face in front of his.

"Don't f***ing talk to me like that," the girl said.

"Stay out of my face, Kim. You're a crazy bitch," Ray said back at her.

Kim . . . her name is Kim, I thought. My mind searched again, trying to make a match. I thought about my old, old, old neighbourhood, where most of my memories didn't make me smile. I remembered hanging out in the laundry room on a rainy day, and sitting alone by the broken swings at Cosburn playground. My world was black and white then, but I was the only black thing in it.

I had been at Cosburn Public School for one day when at lunchtime, I was called a "n*****" and shoved into the boys washroom. They locked me inside. I was scared to call for help. If a teacher came to rescue me, I was sure I would get in trouble for being in the boys' washroom. I sat on the ground and cried.

I heard the door unlock. I jumped up and got ready to make my escape. The door opened and a girl was standing there, jiggling keys in her hand.

"You're lucky I was able to steal these," she said. "I gotta put them back now."

She turned to leave. I followed her down the hall and into an empty classroom. She casually tossed the keys on the desk and walked out. She turned and looked at me.

"Thank you . . . thank you very much," I said.

"You're welcome," she said, smiling. "Well now we can be the best of friends."

Twenty-three years later, I stared at her angry face, shouting at Ray, and I remembered. Now she was five inches shorter, with brown hair and those green eyes. Her face was softer then, almost sweet-looking, but her mouth was just as mean.

"Do what I say or you'll have hell to pay," Kim said.

"How much?"

"What?" Kim asked, giving me a dirty look.

"How much would I have to pay hell?" I asked her.

Kim scrunched up her nose and jumped off the washing machine.

"Shut up Susan, just do what I say."

I remembered us in the laundry room of the 51 Gamble Ave. building. It was the kind of building where no one smiled, and no one took deep breaths of the air because it always smelled like garbage. The six-floor dingy apartment building was where my mother, father, sister, brother and I lived on the third floor in a two bedroom apartment. Me and my "sole mate" Kim were playing in the laundry room, like we always did on a rainy day. My short black hair was braided into little plats with green, yellow, red, blue, and purple barrettes to keep the ends together. I leaned against the dryers watching scrawny Kimmy pacing in front of the washing machines which were practically her height. She was holding an empty garbage bag. I loved watching her hair swing back and forth as she walked. She had so much that I didn't have. She had friends at school, even though none of the other girls liked her. I felt lucky that she had chosen me to be her best friend. Without her, I would have no other playmate but my little sister. I was Kim's shadow.

"Come on Susan, it'll be easy. We can sell them and buy candy."

I turned away from Kim and jumped on top of the dryer. I knew that Kim was too short to get to me.

"I don't want to Kimmy, don't make me."

"Come on, Susan. Do it for me, I'm your soul mate."

"Why don't you do it?" I asked.

"Come on Suzie, I can't do it. You're naturally better at stealing, any ways."

"What?" I said, not understanding what she meant.

"Just do it, Susan. I already told Bradley that

I had clothes for him to sell. I'll make him stop bugging you, Suzie, I promise, but you gotta do it."

The idea of not being bugged anymore by Big Bradley was tempting me. He had been pushing me in dog shit, locking me in the boys washroom, and pulling my pants down at recess, so everyone could see my underwear, for years.

"You promise?" I asked.

"I promise." Kim said, drawing a cross over the right side of her chest in the air.

I jumped off the dryer, thinking that Kim's promises meant nothing. I really had no other choice.

"I'll guard the door," said Kim, handing me the garbage bag, and running over to the door.

She opened it a little bit.

She turned around to see me hesitating by a dryer and looking at her.

"Do it now dummy, someone's coming."

I pried open the door of a dryer that wasn't spinning anymore. I reached my tiny brown hands in and grabbed all the clothes I could hold. I stood up and kicked the dryer door closed with my foot then put the clothes in the black garbage bag.

Kim gestured for me to come to the door.

"Let's get out of here," Kim said.

I was startled by the bus driver yelling for quiet. He was stopped at a red light and was turned around in his seat, yelling down the aisle towards Kim and Ray, who were in the middle of arguing.

"F*** off and we'll quiet down," Kim yelled back.

The bus driver and several passengers turned

around shaking their heads.

Ray and Kim were silent now. Ray sprawled out his arms and rested them on the top of the seats. His legs were open so wide that I couldn't help but look between them. Seeing nothing of interest, I observed the filth covering him. His legs were long, skinny, and covered by grimy blue jeans. His long sleeved shirt looked foul and was covered with his straggly hairs. His hair was as long as Kim's, and looked like it would be as blonde as hers when clean. His face was pale and clean shaven. I avoided looking at his eyes. I looked at Kim instead, amused at how she had changed. She looked like cheap, white trash, I thought.

I surveyed her plastic-looking white heels. A jean skirt was pasted to her thighs. She wore a pink halter top which squished her sagging breasts together. I tried to remember what had ever happened to our friendship.

I could remember my last lunch time at Cosburn Public School. I walked past my screaming, fighting, laughing, classmates towards the fence which surrounded the school. No one talked to me, no one played with me at recess, and no one ate lunch with me. I looked around the playground for my "sole mate" Kim, and found her talking to Bradley and a group of boys. Kim looked up, and mouthed for me to wait for her. Bradley looked at me too, and then I saw him give Kim three quarters. Crossing the field, I went over to the broken swings, and waited while eating my lunch.

I was finishing my salmon sandwich when I saw Kim running towards me.

"Guess what?"

"What?" I asked, wiping my mouth clean.

"Bradley says he wants to be your friend."

I scrunched my paper lunch bag and stared at her. I couldn't believe what I had heard. Bradley, wanted to be my friend? Bradley was the coolest boy in school. He was in the eighth grade, and a lot older than most of the other kids, even in his class. Why would he want to be my friend?

"I don't believe you."

"He does, he does," Kim said. "He wants to talk to you. He's happy that you stole those clothes for him – he wants to thank you."

Kim could still see the disbelief on my face.

"He even wants to bring you to the Spot."

I was amazed. I knew where the Spot was. Beside one of the other buildings on Gamble Ave., there was a long stairway which was entered from outside – when you reached the bottom the door lead to the underground parking lot of the building across the street. But no one used the outside entrance very often, so now the area was Bradley's and his friend's spot. People knew that lots of kids played there, so many of them avoided the stairway or coming through the door at the bottom. It was where the boys hung out and shot caps, or pelted eggs at people in passing cars - the street wasn't too far from the stairway. No girls were allowed in the spot.

"Come on, Susan, please, please go. I promised Bradley you would. I don't wanna look like a liar."

"Are you coming too, Kimmy?"

Kim shook her head.

"I wanted to watch, but Bradley says he only wants you there."

"Why?"

Kim turned around and looked at Bradley, standing with his friends, across the field. She turned back to look at me.

"Come on, Susan. Bradley wants to know now. I promised him you would. I kept my promise to you, Suzie. He won't bother you again; he wants to be your friend."

I watched Bradley smile at me across the field. I smiled back. I agreed to go.

After school, Kim ran with me to the Spot. Standing on grass, we reached the top of the stairs and looked down. We saw him sitting on a bottom step with a friend. They were smoking cigarettes and whispering to one another.

"Bradley, Susan's here," Kim hollered down to him.

He lifted his blonde head and looked up at us. Stamping the cigarette out with his running shoe, he pushed his friend up the steps, and he ran past us, saying hello to Kim. Then he waved us down.

Kim gave me a shove that pushed me onto the steps.

"Go now, Susan. Do everything he says and I'll see you tomorrow."

Kim went skipping away. I could hear the sound of change jingling in her pocket.

I slowly reached the bottom and sat down on the last step. Bradley came and sat beside me. I avoided looking at his eyes. I looked on the ground and saw fired caps, and cigarette butts, and bottle caps. I could smell the underground garage. I kept my eyes on the door. My eyes were adjusting to the dim light. I could see him looking at me out of the corner of my eye.

"Susan?"

He seemed to be waiting for me to turn my head, so I did. I saw that his eyes were grey.

"Did Kimmy tell you that I wanted to be your friend?" he asked, and I could smell the cigarette smoke on his breath.

"Yeah," I said. "I didn't believe her though."

"Why not?"

"Well-I-. . . " I felt confused. Didn't he know how mean he had been to me? "You're always bugging me and playing mean tricks on me."

"That was before, but I like you now," he said. "And I'm sorry for all that mean stuff I did before."

I just hoped he meant it. I wanted to believe him.

"I think you're cute," he said, grinning at me.

I grinned so hard that my face hurt. No boy had ever told me I was cute before.

"Yeah," he said smiling at me. "I think you're the cutest girl in the school."

Wow, I thought. He was being so nice to me. I didn't know what to say.

He stood up and dropped to the floor on one knee.

"Will you be my girlfriend, Susan?"

I laughed at his silliness.

"Okay," I said, liking how that sounded.

I knew that Minnie Mouse was Mickey Mouse's girlfriend. I knew that Daisy Duck was Donald Duck's girlfriend. Bradley would treat me nice. I liked how it all sounded.

"Good," he said, getting up and pulling me to my feet. "That means I have to kiss you."

Before I could say anything, he pulled me towards his mouth. His lips felt cold and wet. I didn't know what to do, so I tried to copy him. I could feel his tongue getting inside my mouth and I pulled away.

"Don't . . . I don't like that," I said.

He let go of me.

"Okay, okay. We don't have to kiss," he sat down on the step. "Let's talk."

I wiped the wetness from my mouth and sat down beside him.

"You've seen a porno film before, right?" he asked me.

"No," I thought for a moment. "What is it?"

He looked surprised.

"Well, it's these films where all these girls that look like you, are doing it with people."

"Doing it!" I said surprised, and giggling nervously. "Where did you watch that?"

"Well, my Dad has a whole bunch of them at home. I watch them all the time."

He kept staring at my face and smiling. I smiled back.

"Do you wanna see something?"

"Okay," I said.

He stood up. I heard the zipper before I saw his pants falling to the ground. He stepped out of his pants and was standing there in his underwear. I looked, fascinated, as he pulled his underwear down, and then stepped out of them. He threw his clothes beside me on the step.

He seemed to be watching my face. I don't know what he saw, but he seemed to like it.

"Wha'cha thinks?"

I was shocked. Just below the edge of his shirt, I saw it. It looked like an elephant trunk, except it had this little hat like the Smurfs wear at the end. His hat was a pale pink, a different colour from the trunk, which was just about the same colour of his pale legs. I couldn't stop staring at it. I had never seen one of those before.

"Touch it?"

I rose up quickly and backed away.

"Touch it?"

"Yeah," he said.

He moved towards me. "You're my girlfriend. You're suppos' to touch it."

"I really don't want to," I said, trying not

to look at it anymore.

"You have to, Susan," he said sharply. "Do you want to be my girlfriend?"

I nodded `yes'.

"Don't you want to have as many friends as I have? Don't you want me to never bug you again?"

I nodded yes.

"Touch it then, Susan."

I slowly reached out my hand and touched it, and then drew my hand back quickly.

"You have to keep your hand there Susan, hold on to it."

"How?"

"Hold on to it like you would a popsicle stick. And sit down."

I sat down. I reached out for it again, this time wrapping my hand around the trunk. I could hear him breathing so heavily. He sounded like he was sick.

"Are you okay?" I asked, looking up at him.

"Yes, yes." he said, catching his breath. "Can you pet it Susan, pet it and you'll see it grow."

Grow? I asked myself. I pulled my hand

away again.

"Susan, don't do that," he said angrily. He started to speak softer. "Just keep touching it. It feels good."

I petted it, and I could hear him making sounds like an animal. I almost thought I was petting Kim's cat. But this boy groaned, and the cat purred. I was feeling like this wasn't right.

Bradley started moving his hips; he

stretched his hands down and grabbed my shoulders. He was hurting me and I couldn't move. I was scared.

"I think I have to go home now," I said and stood up quickly.

I backed away. I hid the hand that touched him behind my back.

Bradley looked shocked. "You can't, Susan."

"I have to."

I turned to run up the steps. Bradley grabbed my shirt and pulled me towards him. My back hit the door.

"You can't go Susan, I paid three quarters for you. You aren't going anywhere."

His eyes looked so mean. He moved towards me. He reached. I screamed as loud as I could.

My mouth was wide open, but no sound was coming out. I felt the tears on my face. I was crying. I looked around and saw a TTC ad, empty plastic seats, and Kim . . . trying to push Ray's sleeping head off her shoulder.

My memory unsettled me, and I had to make sense of it. Three quarters . . . and the old man had chased him away. Three quarters . . . and I had begged my mother to never let me go back to Cosburn Public School again. Three quarters . . . and I went to a different school, made a few friends, and never saw Kim again.

I could still feel Bradley's penis in my hands.

I glared at Kim, wondering how I could have forgotten.

"Do I know you?" Kim asked.

I hesitated, looking her up and down with disgust.

"Yes, you do."

Kim looked shocked.

"I doubt it" Kim said.

"Yes," I said, looking into her eyes. "Yes, you do . . . and you owe me three quarters."

Chicoutimi

I took the few hours' bus drive from Montreal up to Chicoutimi, a Québécois town, to learn French. Before I left I haggled with myself about what to do with my hair. Chicoutimi was not known for being a cosmopolitan place, and I had heard a lot more about it being the heart of separatist politics, than a hot spot for good black beauty shops. The last thing I was going to do was let some white hairdresser who had never even touched black hair before do anything to my head. Wearing braids seemed to be the obvious choice, but I had worn them for years, and frankly, I was sick of the time it took to put them in, the time it took to take them out, and the scratching of my scalp in between.

My decision was clear as I sat on the Greyhound, walkman dressing my ears, bopping my head to Arrested Development's "Natural." There were two other black women in the group of

Anglophones; I noticed them when I got off the bus. The first thing I did was check out their hair. One of them had a relaxer, looked freshly done. The other one was wearing a weave, quite badly done. They were friends and ended up rooming together. They were lucky; they could do each other's hair if needed.

With a pat to my head of twists that looked like they had been done with hands full of thumbs, I met my roommate from Labrador and Québécois mere I would be spending three weeks with. Once we got to the Maison we would be staying at for a few weeks, the Quebecois mere showed us around and gave us the rules of the house. I was cool with all the rules, except for one: we weren't allowed to wash our hair in the shower because it clogs the drain; we had to use a bucket and a basin in the basement.

I tried not to show the horror on my face as I wondered how I would be able to get my hair clean with a bucket and a basin. I needed running water coursing through my tresses, water shooting out of a showerhead massaging my scalp. And at the time, I really couldn't care less about the world's water shortage - my hair needed to be washed.

The next day was the start of the French classes at the Université du Quebec à Chicoutimi. We got a tour of the town and I saw what I expected to see, no black beauty shops in sight. I passed the days struggling with my hair, trying to make it look like it was done with fine fingers instead of thick thumbs. I listened to Erykah Badu's freestyle "Afro" skit for inspiration. Just as I was cursing myself for not sitting through the 10 hours of a braiding session so I could have three weeks of style, and just as I received my 50th queer look from a passerby to my head, I saw an angel.

I was in one of Chicoutimi's malls, walking by a Le Chateau, and I saw a black woman sales clerk (the first one I had really seen from Chicoutimi) wearing beautiful and colourful extensions. I almost knocked over a sales rack racing up to her.

"I love your hair," I said in accented French.

"Thank you," she said in accented English.

"Where did you get it done?" There was such hope on my face as I looked at her, maybe the black beauty shop of my dreams did exist in Chicoutimi and I just didn't know – a little place, just waiting for my business, a place that would give me the freedom to bite my nails again. I had stopped because I needed the length to scratch my dirty scalp. Week two and I was not about to brave the bucket and a basin in the basement.

"I got it done in Jonquière," she said.

Jonquière! At first I thought it was the name of a shop, but I found out that it was a town outside Chicoutimi. I asked the woman if there were any black beauty salons in town, and she answered what I already knew. I didn't have the time to go all the way to Jonquière with the busy schedule I had with the French immersion course. She gave me the number for the hairdresser and I contemplated canceling a weekend of whitewater rafting so I could travel to Jonquière to get my hair done.

Sitting down and listening to Nina Simone sing "Black is the Color of My True Love's

Hair," changed my mind. It reminded me of a fortune cookie I once got and that I keep posted on my bathroom wall, "the first and last love - self-love." For too long in the relationship with my hair, I had made my hair the boss, but it was time to take charge of the relationship. Having fun was more important than getting some fancy hairstyle so I could impress other people. I started to realize how fortunate I was to even be able to go whitewater rafting with my relaxer-free hair, never having to worry about ruining the perm.

On my bus ride up to rafting, I listened to "Natural" again.

The program at the university was intensive, and I had seen my psychiatrist at Concordia before I left. Now I was down to one milligram of Risperdal. I was feeling good. I was playing sports in the afternoon in French, but not being able to hit a ball with a bat. As I had done so many times in the past, I decided to decrease my medication down to half a milligram without consulting my doctor. I had another episode.

My Québécois mere and the other girl I was staying with went off for the weekend to visit some of her relatives. I was in the house basically alone, with one of the teachers from the school staying downstairs in the basement. I had a TV in my room and started watching MuchMusic. There was a video that came on that got me dancing. I was as high as a kite.

"If I could turn back the hands of time" were the words of the song. It got me thinking about everything I'd been through in my life and I decided that if I could turn back the hands of time, I would not change a thing.

I started wandering throughout the house. I opened the medicine cabinet of my Québécois mere, contemplating taking all the medication and committing suicide. I had great paranoia that my Dad was hunting me down. That he had come to

Chicoutimi and was in the house. I went downstairs to the basement where I thought he was hiding and found no one there. The teacher who lived down there left me a note in my *Roberts-Collin French-English Dictionary* that he was going to be out for the night. So I really was all by myself in the house.

The daughter of the Québécois mere lived next door, so I went over to her house, only having met her once. Her children were at home, and they liked me even in my maniac and depressed state. The daughter had to go grocery shopping, so I went with her. While I was in the grocery store, I thought about this show I saw on television once where old people were stealing the lives of the young people who worked in the grocery store. I thought that was happening to me. And I stuck by the daughter, pushing the cart, with her children in tow to stay away from the danger.

By time we got back from the grocery

store, I gave my mother a call from the daughter's house where I screamed into the phone about why she married my father and put me through such an abusive childhood. I was hurting deep inside. And there was no medication to mask the pain.

The daughter called an ambulance and I went to the hospital in Chicoutimi where I roamed around in the emergency room trying to hide because I thought CBC journalists were after me to get the story of my breakdown. The head of the French program at Chicoutimi University came to the hospital and admitted me out and took me back to the school and tried to feed me good food. I had baked chicken.

They didn't know what to do with me. The police came, which I felt safe with because I still thought my father was trying to hunt me down and kill me and didn't feel safe in the Québécois mere's house. The police took me to the police station while they tried to get in contact with my mother in Chicoutimi.

Once my Quebecois mere came back, I was admitted into hospital were I was frightened and scared. My French wasn't good enough to speak to the doctors who knew little English. They put a needle in my bum, which I thought they were trying to puncture my African bum flat like a white person's. I finally went to sleep, because I hadn't slept in days.

My roommates from Montreal got money

from my dad to rent a van and come and pick me up in Chicoutimi. I was supposed to stay there for five weeks, but only lasted three. I still got an 'A' in my French class and accreditation for taking the three week course they also offered.

I finished off the summer deciding to move out from Diane and Alex's place. I found a small apartment in Notre-Dame de Grace.

Elephant Woman

I was having a party for my 19th birthday, and the only present I wanted was Alistar Abego. I wanted him naked and his legs spread before me with a bow on what was soon to be my everlasting chocolate lollipop. But, it was going to take work, and that's what I was prepared to do.

I had seen to it that every liking of his was met when I prepared for my party. I had heard from one of his friends that his favourite colour was green. But even though I hated that colour, I got stomach cramps from blowing up 70 green balloons and a paper cut stuffing invitations in 200 green envelopes. And as I ran around the house picking up fallen balloons, my feet were burning from the blisters I got after spending a day hunting for a store in Ottawa which had the right shade of green cushions to put on my bed. I had run up my VISA bill with the green blouse I was wearing, and the green bra and panties – just in case I got my present.

Alistar, who I met in French class, majored in political science, and I managed to get his schedule of classes by following him around for two weeks. I was a journalism major, I didn't care about politics. For Alistar, I took a crash course by watching CNN and CBC Newsworld every day.

One day in class, I saw Alistar with a *Globe and Mail* peeking out of his knapsack, so I had been reading it every day for months.

It had been four months of almost getting frost bite from walking 30 minutes to school in short skirts on the three days a week I had French class. I spent months encouraging him to call me so we could practice French together, and my hand hurting from clenching the phone too hard every time it rang. Months of living for his compliments, so I could know how he preferred my hair.

Even though it was hard work, it was all worth it to me. My mother would love him. He wanted to be a lawyer, his parents owned three African book stores in Toronto, Montreal and New York, and the family is Anglican.

I waited for him to arrive by the door, greeting everyone politely. I didn't know many of them very well. I had asked Alistar about who he would like to see at the party, and made sure that everyone of them got invitations. So my three bedroom townhouse, which I rented with four other girls, was filled with people flicking ashes to the floor, mashing cheese curls in the carpet with their feet, and turning the beige carpet purple with grape juice mixed with vodka. As I greeted the guests, some handed me gifts. I told myself that I wouldn't open them until I opened Alistar.

The door rang again, I looked at my watch. It was him, I can sense it, I thought, flinging open the door with a smile.

"Happy Birthday!" my girlfriends screamed and threw their arms around me.

I tried to get out of the grip of tacky nail polish so they wouldn't wrinkle my blouse. My friends, Sam and Laura, started wrestling with me in the doorway. They were trying to keep me still to lick my ear, beat on my bum, and tickle my armpits.

"Get off me," I yelled, trying to struggle

away from the feelings of delight and displeasure.

"Okay, okay," Sam said. "The birthday girl has had enough."

Sam and Laura backed away from me. I looked down to take a quick look at myself. My blouse was wrinkled, and I noticed something that looked like a ladder, tearing up my stockings.

"S***, look what you've done," I said.

"Alistar may be here any minute."

I pointed my face to Laura.

"How's my makeup?"

"Smeared."

I started whimpering.

"Don't worry 'bout it," Sam said, taking my arm. "We'll fix you up nice and pretty for your man."

They climbed the stairs to my bedroom.

"My man Alistar," I said, opening the door. "I like the sound of that."

I went to my closet and pulled out my iron, then turned to plug it in, and saw Laura and Sam laughing.

"What's so funny?"

"You," Laura said, holding up a green

cushion.

"When will you stop?" Sam asked.

"When I wish on my candles tonight," I said. "If my wish comes true, I'll stop."

"Why would you waste your wish on a man?"

I looked at Sam with surprise.

"It's hardly a waste."

"Well, if I was you, I'd wish for some brains. All this chasing after a man hasn't done your schoolwork any good."

"That's right, Susan," Laura said. "What are you going to do next year when we graduate and you don't?"

"That won't happen. I could be married by then any ways, and I don't plan on needing a job."

"Right, I don't know how ya gonna plan a wedding. You have no friends," Sam said. "Laura and I are the only ones foolish enough to still talk to you."

"That's not true. I have friends. And you both got a man, so you can make fun of me all you want, but you don't understand what it's like."

I left the room to go wash my face in the bathroom. I moved a *Soap Opera Digest* off the sink counter so it wouldn't get wet;

my place in it was still marked. Those girls are so insensitive, I thought. Laura had a man she had been dating for two years. Sam had more than one man, one in Toronto who she spent her summers with, one in New York who she visited once a month, and one in Ottawa, for a "distraction" during the school year. They didn't know what it was like to be alone.

I woke up to whatever was on the radio, usually some song reminding me that I wasn't the only woman who needed a man. Whitney Houston needed to dance with somebody who loved her, and Mariah Carey called her "Dream lover" to be with her. I turned the music off and eventually stumbled into the kitchen, my short black hair reaching for the sky. The night's drool dried to my face and the "feed me" voices of my stomach loud to my ears. Then I saw one, sometimes two guys, and my roommates, still wearing their boyfriend's shirts. Sometimes one of the guys was making pancakes, but I had to eat cereal because I wasn't the one sleeping with him.

After I had eaten, I looked in my closet and reached for a sweatshirt. But, when I thought of Alistar, I pulled out a blouse and a skirt, and then decided to shower. I would spend hours getting myself ready for school. And when I would run outside and as the bus passed by, so would a car. Inside would be my roommate and her boyfriend, looking warm. Then, I would start the walk to school, because the buses never came when I wanted them to. The wind was fierce walking down the canal, it would race up my skirt, it was the only thing that did, I thought. I would worry about the wind destroying my efforts I made with my hair. But, the only thing that kept me walking was that I was going to see Alistar that day.

I got to school and I suffered through monotone voices and the creak of the wood chairs disturbing my sleep. Thinking of Alistar made me feel better. When otherwise I wouldn't care if my lipstick smeared after eating, I ran to the washroom and reapplied the colour that Alistar mentioned he liked, because I just might bump into him that day.

On those special days that I did, the rush of seeing his broad shoulders and smile made me happy. And when I went home and my answering machine didn't blink, it didn't bother me so much. When the phone would ring, sometimes it would be a male voice, but I told them that I wasn't interested, and unclenched the phone to get ready for Alistar's call. My mother wanted the best for me and always said that sometimes things came handed to you on a silver platter, but you had to work to get the gold, and I only wanted the gold.

I knew that after nine years of marriage, my mother divorced my father. When my father wore a belt, you couldn't see it because his belly hung so low. He used to walk around the house in ripped light blue boxing shorts, which were faded on the bum, worn out from endless years of rubbing against the cushion of his armchair, and wearing away as he occasionally got up to get beer. They didn't always get along.

I couldn't wait to make love to someone again, because all I ever had were a few f***s since I was 14 years old. I was the only born-again virgin I knew. My mother had told me many times that having sex before marriage was like putting on dirty underwear. She said no man wanted to put on a woman's dirty underwear. If it was clean, you didn't get disease, it smelled fresh, and he would respect his wife. I visualized Alistar putting on my underwear and it made me laugh. I had a feeling though that my mother expected me to accept a man's dirty underwear.

I knew there wasn't anything wrong with me. I was not too short or
tall and had great legs and straight white teeth after two years of wearing braces. Hand-size breasts and tasty chocolate

eyes. I had been rejected by handsome men, but they never had a problem with my looks. I didn't know what it was, but my relationships never lasted long, a few months at the most.

After drying my face, I walked back into the room. On my bookshelf, a shiny Jackie Collins book beside the cracked spine of a Harold Robbins one, caught my eye, and I thought I have to start reading that one next time I'm on the exercise bike.

"Girls," I said, breaking up Sam and Laura's conversation. "Make yourself useful. I'm going to have to start fresh now."

I sat down at my vanity table and pulled out my tray of lipsticks in all different colours, bottles of foundation in different shades of brown which I had to mix all together to get my face to match my neck, and cases of eye shadows.

Sam picked up a bottle of foundation

beside me who was sucking in her cheeks, exposing her sharp bones. Sam brushed the liquid onto my small forehead with her fingers, and then felt something strange.

"Susan, do you know there's a bump on your head?"

I furrowed my brows and reached my fingers up to where Sam was pointing. I rubbed it, and realized that yes; there was definitely a bump on my forehead. How could that have happened? I kept rubbing it, with my plucked brows still hovered over my eyes, and then I groaned.

"What's wrong, Susan?" Laura asked from her sprawl on the bed.

"I got the bump when I was in grade nine and fell down in the school's gym area."

"How did that happen?" Sam asked.

"I was wearing five-inch heels."

"I don't get it, Susan. Why would you be wearing heels in the gym area of your high school?"

"Well, Jordie had told me that he liked girls in heels."

"Who's Jordie?" Laura asked.

"He was the guy I wanted back then."

I turned away from my vanity table, and told them the story, hoping that they would admire my quest for love.

In grade nine Jordie Franklin was the one I thought of to get through the day. I had been trying for years to get his attention. When I was in grade nine, he was in grade 13, and he had told me that I was too young for him. But I knew that Jordie liked me.

When I would go watch him play basketball with his friends, he would leave the court just to say hello to me. In the hallways of school, when no one else was around, he would pull me under the staircase and ask me for kisses. I was sure all he needed was to see me wearing five-inch heels, with my long legs looking so sexy, and then he would give up basketball to be with me.

Jordie wasn't on the basketball team, but he went to every game. At the game with all the other girls competing for his attention, I would appear, with a short and tight dress on and my long legs in heels to catch every eye. The only eyes I would look at would be his.

For weeks, I had practised walking in the heels on my carpeted floor at home. When I stepped on the tiled floor in the school, I realized it was hard to walk on stilts on a slippery floor. Jordie never even got to see my legs in the heels, because I fell and hit my forehead against the floor before I got to him. What he did see was my face on the floor, and my short skirt exposing my torn white underwear, with blue flowers.

On impact, the blood vessels had burst in my forehead and when I looked up; I could see the tip of my bump. It wasn't until grade ten when I stopped hearing people call me "Elephant Woman."

After a visit to the emergency ward, where I left with a cold bump covered by packed ice, the swelling went down in a week. But all the blood from my forehead rushed to my eyes, giving me dark purple half moons under them. Another week passed and then to my dread, I had to go to school. And I had to wear sunglasses indoors to hide the dark purple half moons which were slowly fading.

"What did Jordie say when you went back to school," Laura asked between giggles.

"Nothing."

"Susan, you're crazy," Sam said.

"You guys don't understand. You wouldn't understand."

"I've done some stupid things too," Sam said. "But, times come when you know it isn't worth it."

I turned back to the mirror, picked up the foundation, and handed it to Sam.

"Are you going to help me get ready or what? Alistar might be here by now."

I finished putting on my makeup, not thinking about the bump on my forehead, but concentrating on the mark on my chest. A black mark that was left over from six stitches was exposed along with my cleavage. I turned in such a way not wanting Sam or Laura to notice it. That one I got from chasing a boy named Frankie over a fence and getting caught in a loose wire on my way down. The mark was almost as old as I was, well before I even had breasts.

I got up from the table and showed off my face for my friends.

"How do I look girls?"

"Good," Laura said.

"Thanks."

I rushed to leave the room. I was thinking that Alistar must be there by now, and I regretted already not being the first one he saw at the party.

"Watch yourself down the stairs," called

out Sam walking slowly behind me.

"Yeah, and don't get too close to any knives," said Laura.

"Very funny, girls."

Descending the stairs, I saw that the crowd of people at my house was larger. I passed by people spilling beer on my carpet, and butting out cigarettes on my walls. But, I figured I would deal with them after I found Alistar.

I looked everywhere for him. Including leaving the party and going to his house. Like the perfect man of my dreams, he was no where to be found. But I did find him later at a school Christmas party for the French class, and we spent three years together.

Spiderwoman

Roxanne raced furiously to the corner store. She forgot her biology books in the backroom where she had just started working a week ago.

She used her key to re-open the store. She checked the store's clock. It was 10 p.m. The store had been closed for 30 minutes.

The backroom was unlocked and there

was a light emerging from within. It worried Roxanne a little, obviously someone was in there. She picked up a can of peaches for safety.

"Is anyone here?" Roxanne said.

A shuffling of feet was her reply. Roxanne poised for attack over the door of the backroom.

Roxanne almost dropped the can on her foot. The tallest, and most handsome man she had ever seen stood in that doorway, so magnificent, he seemed to be a dream.

This man at the door must have been near 7 feet. The man's dark brown hair curled tightly around his smoothly shaven face. Roxanne had to crank her neck and arch her 6 foot frame to see the man's blue eyes. Roxanne felt dizzy and light-headed. She felt like fainting. She felt as though she were drowning.

"Who are you and what the hell are you

doing here?" the man said.

Roxanne backed away feeling timid.

"I-I work here. I-I left m-my books in the b-backroom. I came back to get them." Roxanne sniffled to keep from crying.

The expression on the man's face didn't change. His eyes bore sharp and deep into Roxanne's.

"I'm Lance, the owner of this place."

Lance turned around and disappeared inside the backroom.

Roxanne followed him inside to search for her books. Just as she was coming in, she tripped on the floor chain that keeps the door open. The chain yanked away from the door and slammed shut.

Lance sprang to retrieve Roxanne from the floor.

"You could have locked us in here. Thank

God that you must have a key to open the door. Now give it to me," Lance said.

Roxanne checked her light blue T-shirt's pocket where she remembered putting the key. It wasn't there. She checked the pockets of her jeans. It wasn't' there. She dumped out her purse and fumbled through her belongings. It wasn't there and couldn't be any place else. Then Roxanne remembered that she changed shirts when she got home. The shirt that she wore all day at work had been soiled by maple syrup. She had forgotten to transfer the backroom key from the soiled shirt to the fresh one.

She didn't' like the idea of telling Lance that she didn't have the key. He could already tell that she didn't have it when she broke into tears.

Lance turned red. "Oh no...we are locked in here. I don't have a key."

"We're only in here until Monday."

Roxanne said.

"You stupid black spook. Remember that I wanted this place closed until Thursday. I planned to go to Mexico with my girlfriend. I don't like my place open when I'm not around. We're stuck in here for four days."

Roxanne's patience snapped. She threw the can of peaches at Lance.

Lance was shocked into silence. There was

peace for almost 10 minutes.

"Give me a hair pin, chick. Perhaps I can poke the lock with it." Lance said.

Roxanne gave him her hair pin. He tried to open the door for 20 minutes, but it was obvious that it would not work.

Lance let out a stream of curses.

"You realize that when you get out of here you will not longer have a job?"

"Yes."

Lance paced up and down. He looked around the backroom, investigated it for any way out. He knew his store too well, if there was any way to get out except the door, he would know.

"I had a great date lined up tonight and all up until Thursday. Sally's the best-looking chick I've seen this year..."

Lance stopped to stare at Roxanne. She was a gorgeous girl, much better-looking than his Sally. He'd never seen a better-looking chick in his life. But, Lance always found a better-looking chick than the last, every week. Roxanne could be the new week's best chick. He'd never had a n***** in his life.

Lance studied her long black hair, hugging her shoulders. It fell gently over her brown eyes in the shape of large almonds. Her nose was so small, it was a wonder she could breathe. Her mouth was rather wide, but in a sensual way. Her colour was so similar to the brown leather in his BMW. Her large breast strained against the fabric of her blue T-shirt. Lance was proud of how easily he was aroused just by watching her.

"So chick, what's your name?"

Roxanne looked up at him.

"What's the point of my telling you? You're

firing me anyway. I really need this job you know."

She was glad that her usual fiery attitude was coming back. Lance the giant no longer scared her.

"It's Roxanne."

Lance was stunned by her rudeness. Chicks were never rude with him.

"Don't be cheeky with me chick. I don't'

take s*** from any spooky dim-witted female."

He picked up Roxanne. She yelled and hit him in the face. Lance reeled backwards, hit his head on the ceiling light then collapsed on the floor.

Roxanne watched Lance fall to the floor with fear. She was scared to see him lying motionless.

She got up and touched his shoulder. He

remained still.

Lance sprang to his knees and fell on top of Roxanne. She fought like a boxer to free herself from Lance.

Lance became very aroused to see her fighting him. She was a sparkler. He began ripping her T-shirt to see her breasts.

It didn't' take much of his strength to rip her jeans. Roxanne fought until her fingers felt raw and her eyes were blurry.

He robbed her.

She sued. Eighty thousand dollars for her pain was her payback. A lifetime of building her esteem was her spider.

Black Hair

Get a group of Black women together and the conversation usually turns to hair.

If I had a dollar for every time I've heard a Black woman's hair story - talked about my own hair - seen people talking about hair in a movie - or read about hair in a book - well, I could buy a lot of hair.

I used to think I was the only one who changed my hair just about every week.

But now I know that many other women have permed, straightened, coloured, cut, lengthened and shortened their hair as often as I have.

When I was a child, my first hobby was playing hairdresser to my Barbie dolls. I grew up in the seventies and eighties but I was not much different from Black children in the forties.

Back then, Black children chose White dolls over Black dolls in a landmark study that led to the desegregation of American schools.

It was not that I preferred creamy white skin over chocolate. It just came down to hair. I wanted straight, long, blonde, brunette or red hair - hair that blew in the wind - hair that I could toss over my shoulder.

And when wishing it didn't make it appear on my head, I used a towel instead.

As I grew older, I spent many years in hair salons turning my head of curly hair dead straight - walking out of the salons with the wind blowing through my hair - and tossing it over my shoulder.

Who says wishes don't come true - for a price.

Although straightening Black hair is known as perming, there was never anything permanent about it for me. There was a war happening on my head. If my hair represented a people, the curly strands were being ethnically cleansed by straight strands with the use of chemical warfare.

Yet despite the chemicals, I've always loved the atmosphere of a salon. In this predominantly white country, Black hair salons create a Black world. During the civil rights movement, North American barber shops and hair salons became town halls for discussions on race relations.

Even now, a hair salon in South Carolina is being used to educate people about AIDS.

Places for hair are no strangers to political activity.

And it is in a salon that I found peace with the politics happening on my own head. Hairdressers looking at my natural hair - and not opening up a jar of Bone Strait - made me rejoice in the hair God gave me.

Professor and author Gloria Wade-Gayles once said "my hair would be a badge, a symbol of my pride, a statement of self-affirmation."

Well, it has taken me a long time, but I finally agree.

Also By Donna Kay Kakonge:

What Happened to the Afro?

This graduate research paper is a strong example of research methodology, case studies and Internet-assisted knowledge that also sheds light on the politics of black hair.

How to Write Creative Non-fiction

Writing is one of the hardest jobs in the world - and this book will give you the help you need to crack the market. Everything you wanted to know about the writing business and how to write with exercises included is all for you.

Spiderwoman

This book of fiction short stories crafted over many years and originally developed in a writing workshop at Carleton University includes the experiences of a young black woman in Canada. Everything from love, to family to tragedy and travel are included.

My Roxanne

Written at the age of 17 and revised later in life, this novel is the story of Roxanne and Lance – an interracial couple who go through their ups and downs.

Being Healthy: Selected Works from the Internet

This book is a compilation of works from the Internet related to health that have been edited by Donna Kakonge.

Do Not Know

This book includes literary collections on madness. A young black woman experiences the challenges and adventures of mental illness.

My Story of Transportation

This book is a memoir of Donna Kakonge's transportation experiences. Everything from roller skates to Jaguars, this is a story of how she has managed to get around.

Draft: spirituality Chats

On a desperate search for a PhD – Donna Kakonge actually produces doctorate-level work by discovering there is more knowledge in one's common sense than meets the third eye of psychics.

Journalism Stories Collection

From newspapers and magazines such as NuBeing International, Panache, Pride, Share and the Toronto Star – Donna Kakonge creates a collection of her journalism stories that span about five years of her freelance writing career.

The Education Generation

Perfect for professors, students and anyone in the college or university system in North America, this book has SEO articles, articles and columns on the education generation.

Digital Journals and Numerology

This book is meant to emphasize how powerful keeping a journal can be with the aid of numerology. I started writing one at the age of seven and keeping a journal has been a constant for me – more than some friends, some jobs and some family members. I used to get a thrill selecting my journals to write in. Now I have decided to try something new by using the computer that I already spend so much time on and money on to show how powerful keeping any journal…even a digital journal can be. Using the principles of numerology can also help in chronicling your life.

Other Work:

"Nine"

This is a selection of some of Donna Kakonge's radio documentaries done with the Canadian Broadcasting Corporation, as well as Radio Canada International.

"Matoke"

This audio book brings the story of Matoke from the book Spiderwoman to your ears.

14 Spiderwoman by Donna Kay C. Kakonge

"Church Sunday"

From the book Spiderwoman comes an audio story of the story "Church Sunday" that was first published in Concordia University's Headlight Anthology and reviewed by the Montreal Gazette.